Music From The Big Tent

Music From The Big Tent
First published in 2016 by
The Dedalus Press
13 Moyclare Road
Baldoyle
Dublin 13
Ireland

www.**dedaluspress**.com

ISBN 978 1 910251 17 1

Dedalus Press titles are represented in the UK by
Central Books, 99 Wallis Road, London E9 5LN
and in North America by Syracuse University Press, Inc.,
621 Skytop Road, Suite 110, Syracuse, New York 13244.

Printed in Dublin by Gemini International Ltd.
Cover image © Christophe Boisson / iStockphoto.com

The Dedalus Press receives financial assistance from
The Arts Council / An Chomhairle Ealaíon

Music From The Big Tent

Macdara Woods

To Charles
with love
Paddy x July 2019

DEDALUS PRESS

DUBLIN, IRELAND

ACKNOWLEDGEMENTS

Acknowledgements are due to the following publications in which a number of these poems, or earlier versions of them, first appeared:

The Irish Times, Prole, Café Review, Poetry Ireland Review, Cyphers, Riflessi Diversi, Stony Thursday Book, Poetry International, Uimhir a Cuig/Numero Cinq; and the anthologies *What We Found There: Poets on the Treasures of the National Museum of Ireland,* ed. Theo Dorgan; *Lines of Vision: Irish Writers on Art,* National Gallery of Ireland, ed. Janet McLean; and *Berryman's Fate: A Centenary Celebration in Verse,* ed. Philip Coleman (Arlen House, 2014).

Contents

II

Epigraph

I DREAMT I SAW MIZ MOON ALIVE …

Thank you for the glory
Of your nakedness
So matter of fact
So wonderful a woman's
Planes and curves
And shadows – breasts
And stomach slope
Legs dancing as you
Talk and pirouette
The secret flash of sex
Nothing salacious
As you say yourself
And nothing salacious
In my response –
Wanting to touch
And see and touch
Because touching is only
A further seeing
With the memory
We hold in our skins –
A kind of wondrous
Punctuation between
Such feelings   emotions
That you spoke of
Learning empathy
As we all have to
From our confusions
Some more than others
Because the callus
In time grows over
All our experiences

And some of us
Were never told how
It really is —
Not the ones who barter
And sell   do deals
And end up where
They aimed for
But those of us
Who had lost our way
Before the plot
Was even broached
Who don't really
Understand the rules
However much
We think we do
Or claim to — there
Is always a key-code
A talisman or ticket
We have not been given
A catalogue
We have not seen
So you work out
A system of your own
A working model
To keep
The whole mechanical
Universe together
To keep the orrery
Going round
But oh my love
The courage and
The wonder
Of the naked body
The bravery

Of breasts and fork
And belly
Of arteries and veins
In the face of time –
On the page
Or in the flesh
From here on in
Be naked for me always
Before memory –
Beyond the bone

I

For Richard Halperin: 2012 *С Новым Годом*

Niall and I walking
Through Perugia
Umbria Jazz
For an evening master class and lecture
By Winton Marsalis
                              When
At the very doorstep of the building
A bird fell dead at our feet
A ragged pigeon it was:
The familiar unfamiliar
From the sky
At the Teatro Morlacchi

Like Marsalis too
Like music – that moment
Between breath and breath
When we must become each other
To keep aloft: keep eye
Contact
Keep time or die

I am in the shower
Reliving this
Eureka moment five days short
Of the Epiphany
After months of silence
And find when I step out
To dry myself
The whole two storeys overhead
Crashed down around me
Water dust and rubble – because
A name so clearly Irish
Is just as clearly Russian:

In one quick tic
From Roman to Cyrillic:

The familiar unfamiliar bird
That fell dead at our feet
Marsalis staring into
The dark arena   your double-jointed
Name like his
Brings back as clear as ice an afternoon
At the Black Sea's mouth
Up the Bosphorus from Istanbul
Alone and drowsy
I sat down after lunch to wait
For the journey back
In the wrong boat
And almost   almost   sailed
Unplanned
At random for Odessa

When All This Is Over …

After all the heads have rolled
and the young men put up against the wall
by the firing squads
when the puppet masters
have taken their seats in the boardroom
and the bombardiers are sipping drinks
with the chiefs of police
when the journalists change sides
and the commentators
redefine what they meant in the first place
and the judges sell their shares
in revolutionary understanding
and the clergy decide
that forgiveness was always for giving
and educators rediscover
the meaning behind the meaningless
when poets grow tired
of too long disputing futility
when the financiers
have poisoned all the blood banks
and the drug companies
have rendered us venomous
when we see that things have returned again to how they are
we want to believe
that the ruthless men in the big black cars
are lonely
there behind bullet-proof glass
and that it means something
that they like us have doubts
in the middle of the night
only worse

because maybe they can do something about it
before the avenging angel
stoops and tears their liver out

Big-Top Music

I've been drunk and I've been clear
I've been straight and I've been queer
I've been young and I've been old
I've been hot and I've been cold

I've been black and I've been white
I've been wrong and I've been right
I've travelled far and I've travelled back
I've been tight and I've been slack

I've been living I've been dead
I've been a mind without a head
I've been false and I've been true
I've been me and I've been you

I've been good and I've been bad
I've been haven't and I've been had
I've been sharp and I've been blind
I've been cruel and I've been kind

I've been deaf and I've had ears
Had good days and had bad years
I've been rich and I've been poor
I've had doubts and I've been sure

I've been mad and I've been sane
I've been marked with the mark of Cain
I've been can't and I've been could
I've been water and I've been blood

/ …

I've been lymph and I've been bone
I've been paper and I've been stone
I've been lost and I've been found
I've been a fox that's gone to ground

I've been ancient and I've been young
I've been a song that never was sung
I've been here and I've been there
I've been him and I've been her

I have come and I have gone
I've been off and I've been on
I've been over and I've been under
Been the taker and the plundered

Been the vanquished been the hero
Patient X and Madame Zero
Been the loved one been the lover
This circus act that's not yet over

Aetat LXX
July 2012

Seafoam

I had been travelling for days
After that
On the spot
And the stitches were working loose
And the citizens
Looking more crossways
Than ever
In their doorways as I passed
                    Until in the end
A stranger took me by the hand
And led me up to the top of her house
Past the chickens and cats
On the stairs
To the space beneath the roof
Where
                    smoking a meerschaum pipe
She picked the stitches out
With a silver scissors
                    Singing as she did:
This is the way that poets die
This is the way that poets die

                    Upon a cold November day
Like froth on a lake
It was – amber and sea foam
Long since gone
With the chickens and the cats
And a woman in a room
And the meerschaum pipe
And those diligent silver scissors
She used
Picking the stitches out of my arm

Sinbad And The Old Man Of The Sea

You can be rid of me
Any time you like
Said the voice behind young Sinbad's ear
But you'd miss
The weight on your shoulders
As I did myself
And all before me
When the time came
            Not so ready then
To say gooodbye
To the two legs wrapped around your throat
Locked at the ankles
And the daily performance
Of finding ways to dislodge me
            Dragging through razor-wire
Lying with buzzards and snakes
Trying to starve us apart
On deserted sea-shores
Or to plunge us both alive
In bog-holes in the wet lands
            There is dignity in work
They say
But I don't believe your heart was in it
And now we're here
At a standstill – at last
Reflecting in the end
On the point of separation
I must confess I'm puzzled   now that you know
You are free to leave
It doesn't seem pressing at all
            Simply unimportant
Or is it just that you have

And know that you have
A newer more valid monster than me
Eyeing the breadth of your shoulders

Surviving

It is the hair and seaweed
Hanging down
The smooth wet bellies of the rocks
That sets it off
The longing and the dizzy leap
From one dimension to another
                    The hunger and desire
I did not understand
The nights I waited for the kind and gentle witches
To come in
Across the city roofs
To join me in my childhood bed
Above the garden space
That smelled
Of Georgian drains
Of unacknowledged ignorance and dust
Impacted damp
And crumbling bricks and slate
                    Curious inventive
Misdirected
Just ahead of where I was
Then – in between
The wastes of innocence
Blind enticing states of guilt
Between the folds of my own skin
My hairless sense
Entwined by rosary beads
Or setting myself alight
                    With sulphur matches – not with sex
Alone and lost
More dangerous yet
Behind the haggard cocks of hay

They never came
Or not in hues
That I could recognize:
I lost whatever end I might have reached
Whatever niche
I might have found
Along the fading road to here:
Odysseus among the ghosts
And ravaged by desire

Disentangling Mars And Venus

1.
I loved   he said   I did
I loved
I loved you as a lover
and a friend …
But not enough   said she
for there were others too
said she
you also said you loved

And then he thought again

of love and loving
and of being   *so easy with*
past nakedness

2.
No words of ours
he said … he tried
again
could bring us any closer than we are

And in the final end of things
there is no need save need itself

3.
But is it *only* sex
she asks
again   *(and God*
how bad is that he thought)
but is it *only* sex
and sweat
and bums and tits

(and that accelerating breath
of impetus   and yes)

4.
It's not like that at all
he says
although it is   bare nakedness
of skin to skin
and for a while to feel
desire   flare up   and die
such hopes
as lie outside ourselves
in the graveyards of the night

5.
A vixen cries
and then …

One dog could find them both

Personal Judgement

In French and Italian
He asked
If I knew the Captain
The Bar owner
The Petrol Station attendant?
        Surely you must know the Captain? –
Or if there were anyone at all
Who might
        Corroborate my claim
To have lived in the village

The Bank Manager
The slow clerk in the post office?
The man in mirror shades
Who cycles everywhere
On the foot-paths?
                        Or
The Doctor
You must know the Doctor
With goatee and scarf?
Or the Pharmacist
Acknowledged by his wife to be mad
But less mad than his sister
Do you not know him?

Then who do you know
Or
        Much more to the point
Who knows you?

And what – if anything –
Do they know about you?

Or – more importantly still –
Choose to know about you?

It was never enough just to be there
Walking the land
Assimilating street-names –
There are obligations
Cog-in-the-wheel observances
To keep the weights and springs
At work
             And you
Were given as much instruction
In the status quo
As any – more than many –
Too much to have come to this

Unknown and disremembered :
Indifference is no excuse
       (besides which it isn't true)
Nor ignorance
And let me tell you straight up   right now
One thing above all –
Being innocent will cut no ice

HOME GROUND

Landing At Logan

i.m. Donald Sur (1935 – 1999)

In the air above Logan
coming in to land
thinking of the last time
and all 15 random checks
that were not random at all:
I'm sorry Mr Woods
but a call has come up on your profile
again
for some reason –
Sorry about that & I don't know why

Maybe because I was short and dark
and bearded then
and noticeably foreign
me and the Russian pensioners
and the Indian woman
with two little boys
even the Sarkozy look-alike
Frenchman
poised out there on the random edge

Take off your boots Mr Woods
Open your belt
Belt up again
Here are your boots

Straight from the X-ray machine
in Cincinnati
for the fifteenth time this trip
easy enough to spot me in Boston
I'll be the one with the glowing feet

Is it true there are two verbs 'to be' in Gaelic
you asked when we first met –
in the Guthrie house
in Annaghmakerrig

It is indeed Donald: and you were both
and I've made it back
to pay my respects
and to leave some books
with poems for yourself and for Wotan's Feast
that last time we gathered
for your nephew's birthday
and the cancer was thieving your life

Isn't that
How our profiles come up

Collins Barracks: Marching Orders

Above the vastness
Of the Barracks Square
The further vastness of the sky:
Eternal invitation to the party with Van Gogh
Without the organ stops
To celebrate the glittering air
Almost too fresh to breathe

But this is what you see
From prison too
Congealed behind grey walls –
To be surrounded by an emptiness so personal
So absolute
That it defies all falling into it
This side of madness

That imaginary place
Where non-existent circles intersect
To leave you
Dropping perpendiculars and tangents
To railway tracks
And tramlines
In the cobbled streets below

The *luas* grand inquisitor
On the tram to Drimnagh:
Howaya Chief ... What age are you?
Not yet old enough I think
For travelling backwards in a stationary chair
Looking out the window
At the garden of the hospice
I am visiting today in Esher

Where everyone is free to walk outside
In summer
Or to be wheeled or walk outside in winter
Well wrapped up –
But old enough that everything that is is perilous
Foreseen and transitory
As guarded as a barracks square

And yet the marvellous wasteful
Momentary roundness
Of the Spring:
A woman running down her steps just now
Across the road
In pink pajamas
All shifting globes and bulbs
And soft tectonic plates accentuated

Seemed airborne in the light of Richmond
Showing for an instant
How it can be done
To be waiting always to be ambushed by surprise
The while
Remembering at seventy to breathe
Each fresh and glittering breeze into the lungs

Members Of The Sheridan Family
In The National Gallery

On detours through the Gallery
From Merrion Square to Nassau Streeet
For years I've been disturbed by this
Unfinished scene of absences:
Three present figures in a sickly shell
As if strayed in from other frames
And grafted here: not family
But members of   Aloof school of   and

You a dying man   perhaps already dead
Before the artist started the commission –
You your brother's wife their son … *I hope
It may engage a pleasing melancholy*
Was Landseer's stated wish –
Blood-distance and disease between
You all and toiling back
To pick up in the Diplomatic Corps

But you don't really look
As if you have the strength for travelling
To keep that certified appointment
In Samara: To be dead this month at thirty
In the British Embassy in Paris –
The strength to face the rush and bustle of the railway
The weather
And the Channel Packet steamer –
Which may explain discrepancy of dates

You look hardly strong enough in fact
For make-believe
To have stepped outside into the garden say

A moment past in
Heavy dressing gown pantoufles and summer hat
And then stepped in again to rest –
Stage properties of nearing death:

The stinking rasp of life is missing
From the lungs –
The minute living forms that drive
The hot-house show along
Are not at work behind the scarlet lips
And lassitude   but the gothic
Sunk-eyed stare is true and fixed on the immensity
Of seeing the rolling spool of light
Run out into the dark of May
And feeling almost there at last
Burial Place Unknown:

The woman and her son
Share in the well-presented emptiness – she
Watches from the far side of the galaxy
Gazette set down upon her knee
Between you and the boy
Who seems to stare as fiercely as yourself
At what it is you see   outside the frame
Where we the audience
Are taking part from front-of-house
In this Smock Alley scene rehearsed:

The painter's landscaped flats
Our dialogue with silence
Not family but members of –
And not a one of us who feels
The rigor and the fever and the intermittent cold
Whatever time we wait

Whether we know our lines or not
And even if we never speak
Or breathe at all
Is ever more than half a breath from it

December 2012

Today I Joined The Company

Today I joined the company
The legion of old men
In Henry Street – the side-door
On the GPO to Radio Éireann
And the ghosts
Where once I was so young
Child actor with the Rep
Ginette Waddell George Greene
Seamus Forde and Brendan Cauldwell
Rehearsing my words
One afternoon in Moore Street
Trying to get the accent right
As I've been trying all my life
To get *the accents* right

These old men today
In Henry Street
Look so much alike – a little
Puzzled at being here at all
Wary of change
Unsure of foot unsure of voice
Not actually deaf
But hard of hearing

Reflected in shop windows
Their images confirm
The X-ray photographs
CAT scans and MRIs –
The fitful
Inner darkness mapped
And laid out garish as you please
A souvenir
All coloured-in in mock relief

Of contoured hills and hollows
That will kill them in the end
This is not what's wrong with you
But what the X-ray shows

The hunter-artists in their caves
Knew all about the beast
The skull beneath the skin
As much as Webster did –
Or the Funeral Home Mortician
Or witch-doctor or the priest
And each of us
Must make its reacquaintance
Walking down the slow
Gradations step by step
Or in a burst of sparkling brilliants
Like the Duchess
Exploding in magnificence
So much magnificence –
And even without magnificence
Uproar of music in the end

Old men today in Henry Street
I've come to love you
Better than myself
In your anoraks and sneakers
Jeans and parka jackets
Keeping out the years
Keeping out the cold
And keeping on forever
Despite the emphysema
The tell-tale heart and the arthritis
The withered dreams
That have at last come true:

And even those secure old men
The years were kind to
Moving up the stairs in Arnotts
Stiffly with their wives
Dressed all their lives
In the psyches of their fathers
Handed down
With suit and crombie overcoat
Fine leather
Self-importance
Signet ring and thinning hair
Pathetic and heroic

Until I almost love myself
For getting up at all – for
Getting out of bed today
For getting washed and dressed
And leaving home – for stumbling on
And turning up
And keeping my appointments
For being here –
                         and being here
Again to see this crowded street

090413

I am 71 today and the heron
Has returned to the park –
In April
Blue-grey camouflage
He shows
Among the cut-back shrubs

Fathers: Revisited

1.
The storm breaks at 4.45 am
I can't wake up
from old exhaustion
and lose the whole weekend to sleep

mid-winter streaks through May
enquiring –
the place you're going to die
have you seen it
have you been there yet

but first explain the truth
behind the curve
that leads us here
to this:
empiric helplessness

2.
1847 in Vienna
Ignaz Semmelweiss suggested
that in beween
delivering babies
and dissecting corpses
doctors should
wash their hands
against childbed fever:
contagion of cadavers

Ridiculed and disregarded
helplessness and anger

grew round him
like a cloak
for twenty years
until he took to drink and sex
to change momentum:
foghorns of breath

In the end they confined him
in a strait jacket
in a mental hospital:
first exclusion
and then irrelevance

Beaten on admission
by the guards
he died of septicaemia
a few weeks after

3
Phil Silvers ... Sergeant Bilko:
sometimes now
we catch each other by surprise
in daytime
polychrome
black and white
and all the Ansell Adams greys
and the room swells
sucks in the light
to bring me back:
Sweet smell
of dark and flickering cathode blue:
late 'fifties
        It was the dust they told me after
when I mentioned that ...

the smell was
Dust collecting on the valves and tubes

4.
Quick-fire sound and comedy
for pirate viewers like ourselves
in Dublin
snow and smoke and ranked antennae:
Empiric ignorance

5.
A bucket of dirty water
he said nightly
        flung into my face
and I'd turn it up a notch
assenting to the fantasy
to put a skin on things
however antic:
Whistler flinging pots of paint
The house that was lost on a hand of cards
The hooded eye of the sniper

The mandolin
for which there were no strings

6.
Unstrung myself
and looking back for explanation
I realise
that this was what I learned
though somehow
not *what I was taught:*
To listen to disembodied voices
in the dark
Not to push forward

To be stoic in defeat
To find objective value
in the damaged lives around me
To know that I was one
and only one
of one   of all
the faceless people
stretching back
to where the world began

that map of loneliness
that cannot be unlearned
that cannot be exploited
      or explained

7.
Rejecting all analysis
I move once more into the optative
rejecting fantasy:

My time among the Isles of Greece
where burning Sappho loved and sung ...

leaving a random crack of window
open
at every last departure:

      Do you remember ...
Remember the day we ... the day.
Do you ... ?
Remember that ... the day ...
his dying words

and
they say that everyone can be replaced

INSTITUTIONS
AND VISITATIONS

С Новым Годом 2014 Счастливово И Мир

Oh little Phoenix
        Who flew here from beyond
And landed easy easily ... *Привет*
        Fionn Uisce ...
Clear lovely water
How wonderful you are
And rare
    So strange
The cartographic corners of the page
Curl in
And form locations for themselves
Like baby-fingers
Imposed on mine
We cross the barricade ...

The little yellow house in Ringsend
Where the pain lived –
Nothing to do with us today
Can't touch you at all
Even without the morphine
The messages in chalk
The medicine cabinet on the wall

Though for a while
(as happens every year)
The lying frames of age and lunapark
Struck up again – again again
the empty *katchmar* weariness
Of giant blue wheel
And whirling staircase
To the stars

(those old prefabricated suspect stars
Of status quo)
Steady and ready to Resume
Same way it always tries –
Invisibly:

this is how it was
it says
and how you wanted it to be

you signed before the mast
it says
to sail the wintry sea

time has yellow teeth
it says
and what will be will be

But then the scratching needle stops
Again (penultimately
But that is still enough)
And like a child
I watch the world come suddenly unstuffed –
The Rule Books and the Form
And me Old Turtle
looking out the window here
Are suddenly adrift
This New Year's Eve:
And everything is possible
On star-fish Kosmos
Commander Phoenix Alexander

Flying *ad hoc* moonchair
Landing slowly

Leaking horsehair and the smell of apples
upholstery and sleep
in not-quite-full control
such laughter and such tumbling
such letting go

and looking down and up – for me –
to see such yet unwritten brand new memories
begin to dust the Three Rock Mountain –
Again to see
the half-opacity of Irish snow

New Year 2014
Hawthorne, St Vincent's Hospital

From The Far Side Of The Styx

A woman came into my room, and sat by me. She came again naked, naked as the day that she was born, more naked maybe because this time it was her concern. Naked, naked: and invisible from the waist down. Which meant that I had nothing to look at there, nothing to be aware of, nothing to be led on by, nothing to be surprised by, nothing to be amazed by, nothing to … nothing … nothing.

The strange figure of the old man who came in this morning, under cover of my shutting my eyes, and deferential, who just leaned over the side of my bed and stood there, with a face of unutterable sorrow, not saying a word, not saying a word at all, just unutterable sorrow, put there by a nurse I think, and then after some time she came back in, said that's all right then now, and took him away and that was it. Very strange.

And the little furry voice, a hairball that runs up one wall and down another, whispering noch einmal, noch einmal.

And then there was the Indian lady, long grey hair, very preoccupied, who came in after my first meal for weeks, stood here beside the bed and pointed to the floor, pointed to the floor we were on, pointed to the floor, and I was watching quite happily. I knew that when I opened my eyes she wouldn't be there, and nor was she. But no matter.

Hazel, St Vincent's Hospital

Staying And Leaving And Signing Out

A Dancing Master in Siena
Half a century ago
After years on top of the Cathedral
Had joints and sockets
Worn away to nothing – sans hooks or grooves
Just old avascular necrotic stone
Cut from the holy body and set twistedly
Anonymous to grace the cloisters
Whispered hoarsely as I passed –
It takes fixity to dance like this

My Venetian Master of the Dance
Is made of flesh and bone
And music in varying proportion
Curiously depending on the time
Of day or night – or even gender
As they told me: so by times
A Prince of amber and the arts
Armed with sword and 'cello
Or else a disembodied lens
Panning across the altar steps
Unerringly
To take her varied place
Among the stone-veiled sybils:
And leaves me with the mystery

My Irish Master of the Dance in Sicily
Was travelling light and wise –
Lighter and wiser than myself
I think today while walking
Up and down St Vincent's corridors
Working a new-fit hip into place:
Lover of Horses and of human kind

He put his faith in wine and song
And iambs marching
Threw his crutches in the tide
Placating sea and hungry rocks
Older in time than God or Purpose
And danced till dawn on a prosthesis:

But that was after – later when
The random blue Ionian wave
(With Icarus again a morsel
To be carried upside down
Mid-speech into the underworld)
Had just as suddenly uncoiled – let go
Drowned ancient sailors drifting up
The layers of myth and pressure guage
The Sirens howling all the way
To this dimension here: where day is night
And night is day and care is simply care
With no extraneous distinctions:

And so my friends we make it
After all
Passing and repassing in the corridors:
Did you ride a bike when you were young?
And where was that?
And where were you born?
Be careful now not to hurt yourself
One step at a time
Better out than in
Good leg to heaven
          Bad leg to hell
And tell me how the world is
          On a scale
of one to ten

January 13th 2014, Cypress, St Vincent's Hospital

51

After Patrick's Day

Long dark winter but
See the plum tree in the rain
A sudden whiteness

March Madonna

The end of March – once more
The springtime has him living rough
Eating rolls and pissing in the bushes –
He tries to light a cigarette
Disintegrating from the damp
And then the lighter doesn't work
His plastic bags and cans and coats
Sit down beside him on the bench

As the Material Girl on the radio
Reminds us – just in case we might forget
Or even doubt that we are truly here
Or that the park is here without us –
That our world is all material stuff
Lacking only things that matter:

There is no material need for Berkeley
To kick the mantelpiece
To make the point – rain
Spitting over Ranelagh
One cold Sunday at the end of March

Salt Fields

Air: St James Infirmary

If you call and still can't hear me
Don't put the blame on me
Here where I always have been
In the salt fields of the sea

Well we got here way too previous
An hour before dawn or so
The early houses still not open
Nowhere else to go

We believe we're somehow stronger
And wiser than before
But I know it's all delusion
And whatever else we were

If you lose her you'll never find her
Nothing but desire
That chains you to the madman
And the ash of last night's fire

Again I hear the loud dawn chorus
Another night has gone
Melted in the blue of the morning
And the great wide world spins on

Well if you call and still can't hear me
Don't put the blame on me
Here where I always have been
In the salt fields of the sea

Grounded

Homage to Eugene Kelly

You Are Here
Вы здесъ
Vous Êtes Ici
But you're not

We can't push
Buttons on
The Metro-map
To light the dots

And if you were
Where am I?
Out on Clare Island
Looking back

Or at red dusk
On planet Mars
Watching those three
Low bright stars

On the horizon
And the lowest
And brightest
Is Earth – is You

Even possibly Us –
But how am I
Out there ... and where
If You Are Here

April 2014

L'honnête Homme

He came
He did the job
Got paid
Moved on

Was what they said they wanted
But wasn't

The Boss's Boy
Was drunk
And a laugh
A silver spoon
In his arse

Not what they wanted they said
But they kept him on

Pro Bono Publico
An unbeliever
Came unasked
As a bonus
A gift from God

Him they kept under lock and key
Under glass and underground

In Spite Of Which

Good Friday 50 years ago
In Seville
I lay in bed in the afternooon
Waiting for my boots
The only pair I had
To come back from the mender's

Today on this Good Friday
I buy a present for my grandson
Whose birthday it is:
And sit in the sun for a while
On a green park-bench
Considering significance

In the shadow of the gate
As I leave
I find a man feeding the heron:
Chicken-leg with the bone intact
And the long beak conjures it away
Down the supple grey throat

As quick and sensuous as that
As smooth
The practiced slightly furtive move
Of pocketing a kickback:
I have to feed him – says the man
Or else he'll eat the baby ducks

Significance or bathos –
It is all I have for the end of story:
A quiet Good Friday
In the blossoming park
And new-hatched Easter ducklings
Unaware of life or death

Cath Chéim An Fhia /
The Batttle Of Keimaneagh

Máire Buí Ní Laoghaire 1822

Beside the river
  In the Glen of The Leap
In the country of Uí Laoghaire
  Is where I am placed
Where the deer goes at night
  For safe repose
Thinking to myself a while
  Listening to the sounds
Of the sweet-voiced birds
  When I heard the tumult
Coming eastward toward me
  Clamour of horses
And the clashing of arms
  Until the mountain itself
Was shaking
  And ugly to us the sound
Hostile and angry they came
  Vicious and malign
Like handlers of poisonous hounds
  An empty bare place in my heart
The good men they left disordered

Not a man woman or child
  But was left shelterless
Crying and keening
  To see the circling militia
Opening fire on them
  Shooting and loading and shooting again

But a shout spread from far and near
        Each Chieftain swearing
He would make trial of it:
        Move sharp there now
The battle has come to us
        Let us be in the centre of it

And they came   the fine men
        I pray joy on the clans of the Gael
Who routed the Fat Swine in disarray

But all too soon
        The violence destroyed us
We were scattered
        On bare earth in the mist
With Barnett and Beecher
        Hedges and White
Coming on in their thousands —
        And leading the pack
Himself Big Barry Bum-Bailiff:
        Oh King of Greatness
May they be laid low
        Without honour or respect
Without worth or harmony
        In the living fire
In eternal agony without relief –
        A hundred great praises to Jesus
We did not pay the worst price
        Of death and reprisal
But lived to make a tale of it
        To be here to tell at our ease

Englished after illness, September 2013

59

II

A May-Day Aisling Skazka

When I awoke that fine May morning
I felt my soul and body turning
to one another with arms extended
back from where they'd lately ended
on an intravenous drip from Lethe
hollow-eyed hung-over sleepy
anxious trembling beads of sweat
freezing in the too high heat

Wondering too how long they'd been
wandering there on Hangman's Green
in the early mist without a stitch
driven by that unending itch
that sets me here and sets you there
and cats in dovecotes everywhere
and sometimes ends in common sense
though mine seems past all penitence

A woman drew over and shook her head
harder to live than die she said
and lies are easier than the truth
with often the same result from both
so open the window now step out
we'll cross the river and make for Knowth
and travel the Plains of Meath again
little red rooster little red hen

Thinking as an old hand thinks
I tried at first to dazzle the Sphinx:
with final end and first beginning
spinning words and further spinning

words of two or four or ten
how we have to go out to come in again
a genie jumping from a bottle
until reined in by Aristotle

⋙

I can't I said I'm too far gone
on the long hard road since I left home
lopped and chopped and rearranged
even the changes have been changed:
Hold on said she hold back your words
come fly with me to the House of Birds
thrushes finches feathers seagulls
hawks of love and tantric eagles

And there in the window where I stood
I was transfixed by a rush of blood
the first sweet feelings of desire
flowed down and up a tickling fire
began to lick across my thighs
causing hope and heart to rise
and everything else as it came to me
that I was naked as so was she

⋙

So too that I was not awake
and since good weather always breaks
it seeming right to sieze the day
she took my hand and we flew away

lifted by our own elation
turning at the Three Rock Mountain
over the fields of yellow rape
watching the season taking shape

A glorious day of early summer
from Hell-Fire Club to Drumacomber
all the landmass underneath
lush and green with cotton sheep
and leaves on trees the wind caressed
so soft and fair and free of dust
affirm that age cannot destroy
the hope of May-Day girl and boy

Ye veterans of dip and dangle
restlesss leg and jig and jangle
here's where the rhythm in the rhyme
turns slower (as will yours in time)
when age comes in so sense goes out
but not the kind of sense you'd thought
and weight of actions good and bad
constrains you like they never had

And fear of course – protective shelf
we raise around the tender self
for few of us at any age
are ready to confront engage
with mockery at all incisive
or even mildly half derisive
and spend too long in our approach
to what we really want to broach

Which simple is as simple does
a tale of gander and of goose
or if you like of goose and gander
or any permutated gender
the *pochemu* of human wonder
is how to know the ideal stranger
however high we hope to go
the farmyard's never far below

And this was much my train of thought
from Sandymount to the Hill of Howth
reflecting how my life's trajectory
not good nor bad but satisfactory
in reaching now three score and twelve
was time to state my *I believe*
and suiting action to opinion
I turned my mind to my day's companion

❧

Who all this time so clear to see
was flying easy flying free
surging onward like a dolphin
remaining every inch a woman
hidden by some screeds of papery
curlicues and hints of drapery
calculated to half conceal
the sinewy litheness of a seal

But to reveal no more than that
except by accidental flash
of nipple thigh or such conjunction
of purpose in a dress malfunction

as she serene and unaware
goes riding through the evening air
allowing those below a glimpse
of what turns men to randy chimps

≥

Her legs were long – and elevation
ensured her perfect aviation
a product of a convent school
she was no timid April Fool
and sought the good in human failings
as magnets do with iron filings
her knowingness was not pretence
and yet she gleamed with innocence

Her principles were inelastic
she saw a nettle and she grasped it
when life dealt her a broken heart
she subsumed it into art
which patched it up and gave it back
and set her on a lifetime's track
of witness as a socialist
and marching with the disposessed

≥

Explaining too how she had been
there today on Hangman's Green
to suport a left-wing project
for putting people before profit
and ceasing from jejune austerity
rescind the status quo disparity
every inch a worthy cause
though not explaining lack of clothes

Left maybe in a bath of Hyssop
the same could happen to a bishop
most likely has but that's another
kind of story altogether
let's take it just for now as read
she'd leaped that morning from her bed
and dreaming at the breakfast table
found her way into this fable

❧

So there we were at least as suited
as might easily be mooted
both with open minds and such
conscious of each other's touch
feeling the breath begin to catch
neurons hurtling in dispatch
the stomach tighten and the blood
circulating where it would

Felt untramelled excitement grow
past measured senses all too slow
forgetting fear forgetting doubt
my psyche showing inside out
and feeling that the time was right
proposed myself for her delight
and her for mine I choked and gasped
in short dear friends I made a pass

❧

At which the Heavens did not split
no God appearing in the cleft
no mountains fell nor seas drew back
the spinning world remained on track

the moon still floated and the sun
continued what he'd long begun
the whisper of *eppur si muove*
was never needed in love's survey

For by its nature love attests
the curving beauty of a breast
the touch of skin and getting lost
within each other's willing flesh
the funny awkward lovely tangle
of lovers trying to commingle
all at once with every part
well hoisted by its own petard

And quoting how the soul transpires
at every pore with instant fires
I turned around to see with shock
a hissing sea-snake on a rock
a gryphon reared with arching back
and talons ready to attack
her voice alone I recognised
screaming from this cockatrice

Of all the mad hesperean wrecks
did you think I wanted you for sex
did you think that I could not do better
if I were looking for a lover
than you you creaking ageing git
who probably isn't up to it
and if you are it's sad I'll bet
I need a man who'll go all night

Six-pack body not too much brain
to make me come and come again
who'll dance me up and dance me down
dance me out across the town
with fireman's thighs and fireman's lift
glutes and pecs insanely ripped
and agile too with gorgeous cock
I want a man who was built to fuck

And if he isn't up to snuff
I shall destroy him quick enough
for his presumption in my bed
I'll kick him out upon his head
presumptive feeble and not knowing
when and what he should be doing
one whom I can tear and scratch
and break upon my torture rack

                           ❧

I don't have time or will to ask
or slowly show – still less to teach
and there you go I've said my bit
so tell me what you make of it:
Well yes I said it seems on balance
your discourse is made up of challenge
so too by implication threat
but there's life in many a quare place yet

And how could men not be dismayed
to see their privates on parade
snorted at in clique derision
by the latest empty-head division

not quite hell-o-oh and oh-my-gawd
but even worse because of fraud
this father and mother of all apalls:
ballsy women with cobblers' awls

              ~

And I believe a better challenge
is to lie together and see what happens
for yonder all before us be
deserts too vast for you and me —
to lie together without a script
not even trying to remember it
the only rule to make allowance
for what preserves the human balance

And human does as human goes
frequently steps outside the laws
gets things wrong and makes them right
then wrong again and tries for truth
asking only human warmth
to exercise each human warrant
and at the centre of what's natural
to worship at the tabernacle

              ~

Co-ordinates of first and last
the portal through which all have passed
the initial truth we each must learn –
there is no prospect of return
no way back into the garden
we left without parole or pardon
or even from what point we start
our journey between dark and dark

And separating love from lust
(like separating mud from dust)
depends on humours wet and dry
in the end you'll ask why bother why:
it can't be done except whenever
chance and weather come together
and Janus if he's liberated
cannot hold on to both his faces

And now at this end of the joke
the coming storm begins to break
to have grown old is not a crime
tell those who live in Hangman's Green
we flew off once we can again
smell new earth in the drops of rain
but now give over run for cover
not even May can last forever

15 – 22 Bealtaine 2014
Hawthorne Ward, Saint Vincent's
& Fair Belmont, Dublin

PICKING UP

Sons Are Older At The Speed Of Light

I.
My father did not finish things
Such things as rows
Or playing parts   And breakdowns
Retiring early   Died too soon
His final words to me – A
Half a question   Half unasked
At no point answered   Comes there
Any answer ever?   *Do you ...*
Do you remember ... When ... and there
It stops unfinished in my head
Do you remember when we ... Lost
The points of contact maybe
Or lost the faith   Or lost our nerve
Lost certainty along the way
As is the way of things   And now
That I am gathering speed
The train tracks meeting in the distance
Far behind   The fearsome nameless
City rearing up in front   where I know
No one   and none know me
But where we all get off
It is too late to even think of asking questions
And of whom?   The young Eastern
European with the tea-urn
Has passed up and down the corridor
Three times   has disappeared
And gone for good
As has the man who checks the tickets
And the district nurse   who is
The only one that anyone could trust
Out of the whole shebang and calaboose

Or – to use my mother's phrase –
The Slaughterhouse
This travelling slaughterhouse on wheels
We call a life
                    But not an unconsidered one
Out of the four last things
This one remains   Impervious to fashion
Time or doubt: the flame   it flickers
And goes out
The bird across the banquet hall
No more than that
                    And yet we
Mostly   stand our ground   because
It is expected
And what I am trying to understand
Even now at this late hour
Is your unhappiness and thus my own
Beyond the dopamine deficiency
And those endorphins
Creatures of the vasty deep
Who do not come when they are conjured

II.
Yesterday I climbed   lungs heaving
Up the earthquake damaged street
                    Nocera Umbra
Much   *chiuso per restauri*
And simple minimal   so beautiful
So free of traffic   free of noise
Mid-Wednesday afternoon
One self-conscious policeman
Checking doors so tightly shut
Not even dust could penetrate

75

And near the top
Two men are laying cobble stones
In sand   tapping them square
Into the roots of time
In shadow
In the lovely buttered honey light
Of mid-September
                        This constant need
For rehabilitation   Spells in John of God's
Cataracts removed
Appendices
Colonoscopies and cardiograms
Or how in 1991 in Moscow
So many Metro escalators stopped
Seized-up   steep egress from the underworld
Sotto Restauro   everywhere *Ремонт*
Remont   we climbed up from
The marble bowels and chandeliers
Of Kruschev's dream made real
But lacking maintenance
The way we do not finish things   is
Where entropy comes in   is Auden's
Sinister cracked tea cup
And the Watcher in the shadows
Who coughs when you
                        would kiss
Or coughing   labour upwards
On a stick and artificial hip
To the Civic Tower and campanile
La Campanaccia at the top
Built nine hundred years ago
And standing straight   full weight
Erect proclaiming   *Eccomi*
For I am here and have been here for all to see

And have been seen
                        As I too am here
And have been seen   been part of this
Small space today between the Tower
And the cathedral
All *chiuso per restauri*   Have seen
The maintenance and putting things
In place   Knowing that they must
And will go wrong again
And be put almost right again
Poor transients –
Until the Heracliten lease runs out

III.
And one day indeed the words ran out
And we   with nothing   left to say
Consulted over menus
Read bits of news   repeated saws
To get us through the silence — you
Didn't know
                    And I had yet to learn
That few words   A simple few
Could be enough   could tell it all:
A tendency to stagger to the left
And sometimes teeter backwards
Which could explain
My dreadful fall in Fiumicino
Too much saliva
Varied tremors   Hands and chin:
And sometimes fingers clawed
In sudden spasm
                Do I go on
Into the realms of dysgraphia
Staccato speech   Shoulders stooped

A slowing of the gait?
I prefer
To watch the dancers in the village square
The *ballo in piazza*
Sunburnt mirth   Provencal song
That so caught Keats' fancy
Out of reach
And I have had a longer run than that

And not yet reached Astopovo:
Still travelling
                    To places all unseen
Invisible to those with open eyes
It needs a certain antic 20 20 vision
To housepaint in the dark
As we have done   And plastered walls
Without a light in Fontainebleau
Not cowboys then or now
Just battling with addictions
                    Drink and pills
And work   At labouring   And selling
Two hours of life to buy a third
The hell with that bum deal
I said   And I have now grown old   And someone
Cooked the books
                    Along the way
The way we knew they would – So
Who owes what to whom is moot
Irrelevant   We last from day to day
No more than that   That's it   Enough
For now
The diagnosis works   Of course it does:
Who ever died a winter yet?

September 19th 2014

Dream Song

Nor would Signorelli do a Perugino rolling eye
As darkly, sometimes, Heinrich did, alone,
Orbs ascending in fierce frenzy, neither love nor ether
Could assuage: he walking bareassed
Up the stairs, come small hour, two a.m. Old burns
Upon the knees and elbows. Of his skin.

After, O too many, years to come to this, unstable
Naked exile, he knows, that transience is all,
& all is vanity, & that standing still
And moving on are much the same:
And matter less. Depends,
At base, on where you're looking from.

The monster in the morgue had monstrous rings
Made from glass eyes of the dead. Finer
To fondle wounds & larval mouths & eyes: & after death
The blow-fly, truth. Ovid, could read,
With the soles of his feet: O, well enough,
At least, to keep the traction taut.

Old Men

for Jo Slade

That universal
Just-now veteran
On Via Filosofi
Stepping downhill
In discomfort –
I see him
Everywhere I go
The same unaging
Puffy face
Grimacing to
Catch his breath
And also
Because his feet hurt
But he always has
An assignation
Always an appointment
To be kept
In some decided
Rendezvous
With some minor
Daily business
Which must be done
As well as – more
Importantly –
His Free-Travel
Medical card
And weekly visit
To the District Nurse:
And sometimes
He grows fretful

About such things
The thousand
And three intrusions
On the day –
Even before
You take on board
The Parkinson's
The Emphysema
And Angina
His over-taxed resources
Spread too thin:
Until I then recall
How such old men
Can pull
The strings of history
The post-war gothic
Images
In Black and White
Of those two
Sabre-toothed wolves
In Yalta
Carving up the kill:
While in between
Frail and weary
Roosevelt sits
With cigarette
And cape
Trying hard it looks
To be there
But not quite
Able to keep up

Song For The Magic Mountain

In Istanbul I bought a shirt
And shoes from Cesarini
Set up shop as Hans Casthorp
With partner Settembrini

In Anglesea I disembarked
Migrating south to pasture
Until I came to Marble Arch
And fields of alabaster

In spring I started up again
On a wind that blew from Ealing
Soldering for Sir Christopher Wren
On the pipes above the ceiling

In Avalon there is a road
And a house marked number seven
Ruled by eighteen stones of Flo
And justice most uneven

In Ladbroke Grove I came to rest
Weary undecided
Until the night we burnt our boats
On bad lysergic acid

On Dover beach I tried to sleep
As I took my leave of England
But as ye sow ye so shall reap
Of cold and stony shingle

In Salamanca I took note
Again in Rome and Paris

The sense of purpose that had built
Each exiled Irish College

The sun arose in Lavandou
Above the Bormes mimosas –
Off-red and white – that lightly strewed
Confetti on the roadway

A job came up in Zonguldak
But I was back in Dublin
A loaf of bread a jug and cup
For drinking tea and jasmine

Amor vincit omnia
Throughout the National Gallery
We know however staid we are
There's truth in all tomfoolery

My shirt I bought in Istanbul
My shoes from Zugaroni
A monkey suit in Hartlepool
And a ticket for Mahagonny

My Degas Words

for Eileene McLoughlin

Would you dance
for me
in an empty room

With tall windows
high ceilings
and a mantel-piece

Bare boards
A door
onto a staircase

And nothing else
but silence
and the physicality

Of flight –
the weight of breaking
free and falling

Back again
as if suspended
in a mirror

The floating
rocketry and stamina
of centuries

Which I so want to see
up close
because it looks so easy

From afar
as all art does – except
for love

Which seldom can
survive
in time and distance

Without its own
delusions
its own constraints

In Tomis He Remembers

Is this how we end
In distance
You are all too beautiful
I am too old

Long cactus years
And roads
And brutal corrupt politics
Have intervened

Time is distance here
True distance not
Spiny silence between
Place and place

And where you are
Such closeness
As still gnaws at me in age
Untouchable

And longing to be touched
Again
Just one time more
Before it ends

Too old for that rich milk
Of almonds
Too late for phantom cab rides
With your lovers

Nature Non-Actuel

Of course the picture
Does not can not stay the same
But something does:
Charlie Butterworth butcher
Barrow-on-Furness 1890
Gazes out as prime as beef
Red raw steak and bone his cheeks –
A moment that does not stand out
From the hackings and scrubbing
Of his life   his wooden benches
Work-tops   little balls of meat
That roll and stick and end up
Slimy fibrous   On the floor
And always cold
The cold of death beneath his
Well-scrubbed woodrubbed fingernails

And if the picture does not change
Then where is
Van Gogh's postman
And Goya's moment of himself
Desiree Dihau reading in the garden
Or Pierrot or Columbine
Working
The quick-change costume switch
In some improbable
Commedia del Arte
Square in Cumbria –

They occupy the same space
In the air
As the uneaten phantom pig
In the shadows

When Judith Herzberg
Stopped eating pork
In later life
Starting a line of shadow pigs
All witness to the fact
That post and propter
Have little to do with it
That everything dies anyhow
And when we stop we stop

And that Dutch
Farmer who gave a Jewish
Poet shelter eighty years ago
Did or did not live to see
The whole world overrun
With hazy shadow-pigs
Reproducing daily
In every phantom guise and species

And Charlie Butterworth
British butcher
Barrow-on-Furness (1890)
Is there forever
Hope and Glory
Flecked with saw-dust
Smelling of meat
His hair the colour
Of his well-scrubbed blocks
And no one will ever
Know him else

Old Eben Flood And I

Old Ebeneezer Flood
And I
Well learned the sound
Of closing doors

Knowing in advance
Who would
Lose us overboard
And who would later turn

Their heads away
When they
Might see us board their train
Or walk into a room

I don't remember that
They'd say
I have no recollection
Absolutely none

Are you sure that
It was me
And if it was – then are you sure
That you were there yourself?

Bob O'Donoghue spoke only
Simple truth
The day of the Great Book
About finding long-lost poems

Waiting quietly in the blood
And how he didn't need

To let on to be half-mad
To find them either

Just rightly mad enough in fact
To first presume
To break the silence – and then
To go on breaking it

Unlicensed and without permission
But this is something
That can take
An unrewarded lifetime to discern

Cannot be truly learned
Until too late
It needs the certainty
Of seeing the Steamer all lit up

And setting out to sea without you
New sailors
On the bridge inventing latitudes
That you've already mapped

Poor Sisyphus and friend
Walking the avenues at night
And climbing up
This hill above the town

Looking back to check the road
By which we came
The years we lived to reach
This place where we now rest:

And Mr Flood if you insist –
I'll put it into words
And you can sing –
How we so wanted to believe

That playing to the gods
With the fantasists and faux amis
Seemed better
In the end than not –

To use the freedom to be wrong
Strips any claim upon
The careless
Carefree islands of the young

The Most Beautiful Woman in Dublin

In the Park today
They are speaking
In Russian – I hear them
Muscovy people to
Muscovy ducks
And the homeless man
Who sleeps here rough
Is pumping weights
One hand at a time
All doing our best
To try and get fit
And some are too old
And nearly bet
On the circular paths
Around the lake
Self-serious pigeons
Posture and strut
While outside the gate
In the sun after Service
The Adventist faithful
Spilling out through
The Temple Doors
Are suddenly turned
Into Sabbath flowers
And the Persian owner
Of the Carpet Bazaar
Across the way
From Village Books
Up in *Kutubiyim* –
The Marrakshi street
Of a hundred
Bookshops –

Waves at me
To come on over
Have you been ill
He whispers – You
Haven't been round
As much as you used –
Solicitous too
He sells me a cane
Easy to see
Too short for purpose
And says
I'm to mind myself
For these days even
Seventy
Is still too young …
Too young too old
Too old   too young
Until I behold
In the Ranelagh delta
The One
Most beautiful
Woman in Dublin
Toyin Odelade
Carrying a ladder
Arrayed and clad in
Fabulous light
Bathing and glittering
Corruscating
The whole of the SPAR
INSOMNIA and
What was the CENTRA
Outshining the waves
And rays of light
Reflected – even with
ice ice baby advertising

White on blue
Commercially lettered
Across her breast:
Today I'm a slogan
She says –
Putting things right
Before they go wrong –
But isn't the Sun
Today Magnificent?
And just for a while
It is summer in May
And nuts in May
And all the way
And years
Of summer to come
For just that moment
As every year
We again discover
All May beginning
And ending never

May 2013

Nerium: Hiroshima Day 2015

Shadows in the morning
Make cathedrals in the yard
Buttresses and spires
Display along the pig-sty wall
The steps and the cantina
In angular contortions –
Shoot acrosss the well-house roof
Aimed by the climbing sun
Until the oleander flames out   so pink
And old and shocking   all at once
So intimate and so reserved
I never knew till now
About the legacy of dogbane
A toxicity so fierce   100 grammes
Could kill a horse   no part
From crown to root innocuous:
For more than thirty years
It has been there   familiar   innocent
Sometimes exhausted by the heat
And waking in the cool at night
Oleander swims the Bosphorous
To carry back the mouse-moth from the moon
And Catherine Queen Butterfly
To join the flying whisks and whirligigs
Of insect life in Umbria

                    They too must live
As must   the boar   the nutria
The archer porcupine
Brought in before the flood
To swell Trimalchio's menus
Of larks' tongues quails and dormice

Sometimes now on the roads at night
We see the family convoys cross
From one tilled field   onto another
Chewing and grunting as they go
Content and immemorial
As strange and socialised as geese
Those cackling guardians – for
Whom intent and instinct mixed
To warn their sleeping owners of attack
Unike the oleander which is
Simply there   and everywhere
And travelled here
From everwhere at once
With all the symbiotic presence of a cat
So wonderful it is not seen
Until you've almost passed it by
A humdrum flash of pink across the street
Or occupying someone's garden
As an afterthought   it almost seems
A poster for a concert that has been
And gone   all done   and yet
Will come again   somehow   the same precise
A rusty silent seized-up clock
In a hedge
That tells the right time twice a day

                    And keep
The dog far hence indeed   *Apocynaceae*
Stuff of urban legend   classic lore
Whole dynasties destroyed
You might have made it into walking sticks
Perhaps   in lieu of olive
But not for skewering meat
Nor yet for building fire to cook

Poised wooden toxic garden-horse
About the house
We so surround ourselves with death
Laburnum   deadly nightshade
Yew   tobacco   lily-of-the-valley
None looking so at home
So much a relic of old order
Half stories half-recounted   old decencies
Of putting *smacht* on things
Trimmed paths and summer afternoons
And all the faded latest   songs
Played on wind-up gramophones
In the years between The Wars

        Salted mushrooms on a tray
Set out in the sun   upon a hedge
Was what I saw   Suggesting yes
With linen   airing   and the cavalcade
Of peoples coming down the years
The tinsmith and the egg-man
Turf from the bog   hay-bogies
Rolling low to the ground
From distant fields   mysterious
Spools bobbins and a sewing machine
Box-cloth and box-wood   Strange
Frieze   my grandmother a girl again
Her parents in New York
Crocks and churns and shiny delph –
Keeping all one's horses in the air
Such memories that are I feel
Of things that never were

                But being true
To them without traduction   untranslated

Images   is how the poetry works
And how the tangent comes to touch
Some point of contact   that fires the spark
And drives the process on
An oleander in a sunny yard
Where children safely played   Were children
Ever safe   I ask   instructs us too
Of how   our cells   are split
One from the only Other   and how we go
How murderous   That young girl
Naked in the road in Vietnam
Still burns and will until the oil burns out:
This unassuming pink and poisoned
Travelling Asian flower
In August nineteen forty-five
Appeared in the shadow-land
To claim its own – and speak
For what had been Hiroshima

FLYING
WEIGHTLESS

Vivre Sa Vie

1.

Òu allez-vous comme ça
Is what the polis asked
On the road the morning after
We'd slept in the heather
Near Castellane
Bag and baggage and young
Our bedroom ceiling
The open sky over Var
October windows on the
Coming winter: *comme ça*
Òu allez-vous   comme ça
As if we knew   as if a passport
Offered explanation
We were there   just there
On the morning after
Under the mountain
Where we slept in the heather
Under the open sky of Var
Where fifty years ago
We were and somehow are

2.

C'est lui le chien mechant?
Asked the Belgian earlier
Nodding in my direction:

Out walking along the Seine
On a break from our room
Like everyone else

Even the smart-arses
From the Aesthetic Faculty
For once seemed almost human

And I recited Yeats'
Song Of Wandering Aengus
To prove that sound

Could get around language
That meaning could go
Into town and back

In the open space between
The words
And then the Belgian started

All humped up
Like a ticket inspector
In blazer and slacks

C'est lui le chien …
Non c'est lui
Le mauvais garçon

In the schools they teach
Explication du Texte
To one and all

Enlightenment rolls in
Like dawn
Or the men in caps who clear

The penniless sleepers
With nowhere to go
Out of the empty railway stations

Into the streets
And history is only
The movement of peoples

3
Now that I have turned my back
On all currricula
The scrabbling and scratching
And self-importance
I see that what I was being taught
Was cloning   To choose a name
From the menu
A myth that would fit   With the others
And make it my own   As it were
And thus preserving
The state of disciplined exploitation
In which we vote and float –
As predatory social beings
As the man behind the Orchard Bar
In Delgany knew
Don't come back don't ever come back
He told the Henrys   then added
And that goes too
For your Pakistani friend
Sending the message to me
Like Queen Victoria's gunboats:
You can't do that there here
But we can do this here there
Sure as hell   If we want to

4.

So many facets to memory –
Recognizing a woman's foot
In a brown shoe
In the Gare d'Austerlitz
And not looking any further …
My next point of contact is
Walking one side of the nightmare
In the voyou country
Around Cardinal Lemoine
Didn't expect to be
Walking the streets with a razor blade
In my pocket
A monster on my arm
Not even sure how to use it
The rules of engagement
But I knew when it came to it
As it seemed to have
Whatever happened
I was there in the wreckage
Which is how people come to be
Doing life or forty years or dead
But this is what you learn after
Too late to be of use
Old Dry Man as John Jay laughed
Reading the label
On his bottle of African hooch
And dying some weeks after
Of a heart attack
Five winners up
At a Wexford Point to Point
And today I am sitting on a train
Generations later
With a *tableau vivant* of memories

Played in house-lights
And starting out awake each morning
Still making north for Rouen

Il tuo amore era bello

Which translated
text   You asked
first took me
heart and soul
into another world

And my answer always
that same Satyricon
I read in French
in August heat
in Paris and in love

In nineteen sixty-one
another country
and besides …
I was transported
transubstantiate

Cared not a naked rap
for Port-Royal's report
that pagan love
and life can only end
in loneliness

Celibate horror
at the phallus in the garden:
I'd rather have
Ruth Brown or
Lucille Bogan any day

Who knew what they
were at and why
and what was what:
If I can't sell it
I'll   sit on it

Inalienable Ruth
who made them laugh
in the barrel-house
small hours
with the doors closed

We most fiercely
want that
which we cannot have –
is our insurance
in a big bad world

Addesso é brutto

It is all translation:
tears to music
certainty to fear
speech to silence
and energy to age

Not even a rocky
outcrop
to distract us
in our returning down
into the plain

Hot sunlight
making shapes
of dust or haze
of sleepy breasts
and slopes

As we begin to die
inside   the day
we recognize
that we no longer
truly hope

For afternoons
of stony pathways left
to stumble down
δε δοχμια in code again
and Spanish boots

Strozza Capponi at Seventy-Three

Air: The Limerick Rake

What was it John Jarvis
What was it you said
As I walked through the site
And you paid little heed
It was easy to see
That I hadn't a screed
And you wouldn't pay much
For my labour

You told me of rainstorms
That soaked to the arse
And you just sixteen
At the bricklayer's trade
So it's strange now your present
Is turning to past
You renegue on those young
Days of labour

The Hammersmith gaffer's
A weaselish gent
As he stands with his watch
On the edge of the trench
Till one day he fell in there
Without his consent
For fiddling
The roster and wages

The men on the pre-cast
Eat thick bloody steaks
Which they fry up afresh
At the midmorning break

While others slope off
To self-medicate
And get rid of the shakes
In the morning

And that's how it was
In my halcyon days
Weekends of cash
For ironic display
Of a Saturday lunchtime
Down Notting Hill way
At large with the rich
And the famous

Now see there Jack Doyle
With a flower in his coat
Making for Finch's
To take up his post
All my childhood in Dublin
I'd heard of exploits
And disputes of himself
And Movita

And one day I bumped into
Young Charlie White
From Ballaghadereen
And late of Westport
Hand turned to podiatry
Writing the life
Of the genius that was
Little Richard

They come and they go
And they go and are gone
Pale rider among them
Is Jeremy Swan
Whom I first met in Achill
The campest young man
Who laughed like a lark
Out of mourning

The truth is I fear that
There is no escape
Like the man who got trapped
In the frame of the hoist
And hung on there screaming
Held up by a rope
While they worked to uncouple
The housing

Except maybe love
If such love could be found
As easy and free
As it once did abound
To grow and to greet
And to heal and astound
Our poor hearts and our lungs
In the morning

And what if it's true
That such love is no more
That it's time to give up
At ten and three score
That good-natured women
Should show you the door
But are so far too kind
For to do so

And as gilt on the lily
The dopamine patch
Sets you off like a lemming
For gambling and sex
If you were not before
You're now down on the list –
Old men who may be
Inappropriate

So I'll wander the roads
For as long as I can
Remaining a hopeful
And upstanding man
To find out the ultimate
Terminal plan
Of the butterfly and the
Red rosebush

Ceangal

Granda has gone for a walk in the park
To see if the alarm bells work
Then he's away to the hall of the winds
To pray fair weather for kith and friends
Climbing up to the top of the stair
Breathing hard in the thickened air
And harder still in the silent fear
This time next year he won't be here
In the afternoon he slips into bed
To close his eyes on General Dread
And those enforcers – Doubt and Sweat
Who work us sore both day and night

Hand to plough and lip drawn back
You may well find him in the park
Leaning hard on his holly-stick
A Christmas gift from Derryhick
Sent with a Carricmacross inflection
To mark the Kavanagh connection
With sheen and turns and lovely throat
Uniquely chewed by a Mayo goat
Essential now as an all-in-one
To a man who is living with Parkinson's

He may even call to the place of flowers
Depends on the volume of passing crowds
And if he does he'll buy fresh blooms
To put in all the Selskar rooms
For colour and life – though not for smell
For scent and essence no longer tell
Of stolen shoots old heroes won
The fragrant fruit trees of the Sun

Transported here from the golden sands
Past Kazakhstan and Samarkand

Like an ancient train on rusty points
Changing gears on jerky joints
Sleepers loose on sunken gravel
He must each day again unravel
What plans if any have been made
If they should be at all deferred
Identifying each new pain
Losing force and leaking steam
However hard we feed the fires
What should take no time now takes hours
Between the fumbling and the doing
Starting out and then returning
Stopping short and made to wait
Until the back pain may abate

Or yawing widely in the street
An empty sail-boat gone adrift
Turning round without direction
Of pilot rudder crew or captain
Remembering when we break the pause
Big steps big moves big breaths big voice
We must keep moving come what may
In order to get under way
Or even out of bed some mornings
Those disregarded childhood warnings
On making faces without thought
If the wind should change you'll be left like that
And so it did and so we were
Falling into the midday hour
Backwards through the empty air
To crash at the foot of the airport stairs

(And that was a crash at sixty-seven
Even before the medical cretin
Doctor in scrubs and perm and Title
Came on at eight all primed and fighting
Clearing out us day-time gifts
For a peaceful orderly night-long shift
An obsessive evening ritual labour
Of emptying 'his' Augean Stable
Ejecting all who took his whim
That they might sink or they might swim
No bella figura – *but louche* disgrazia
Along the darkened shore of Ostia)

But to continue my half-mock redaction
We must avoid all such distractions
Be mindful of our hands and feet
And how we place them on the street
Remembering too to swing our arms
And to be careful how we turn
Or stretching upwards to observe
The flow of traffic from the kerb
A moment of stray thoughtlessness
Can cost you dear – a broken leg or humerus
Some lasting harm which in the end
Means going back to start again
And over days and weeks and kalends
Reorganising how to balance

And for the moment so it goes
Thinks Granda walking up the road
And how he with a little luck
Will make it up to Village Books
Where kindness is and elephants' feet
Provide a perch to sit and read

115

Become acquainted with those tomes
That he may later carry home
Which really isn't very far
You know … the bridge that isn't there
As it was known by all of us
Before the coming of the luas

The problem is how long and far
He now may reach in going abroad
He could fly to Rome in a lyric burst
But would Rome become the terminus
And for how long can he remain
At large and going from town to town
Through strange intricate alphabets
Like Dublin with its minarets
At the Pigeon House for all to see
But still for most a mystery
As poetry almost always is
Simple urgent and mysterious
But to go to somewhere further say
Like Indonesia or the USA
Or even with a touch of brio
Raffishly to make for Rio
Or set out again for Buenos Aires
A place for charging poetry batteries
Where bravely and without apology
They made a splendid verse anthology
Exchanging bee-loud lapping lakes
For Irish sea-foam on the Plate

Time is distance after all
Stretched between birth and funeral
And even your Romesco cabbage
From close-up seems a perfect Sceilg

Which form it so completely apes
You could defer on rules and tapes
And there's no measure to assuage
The changes that arrive with age
And worse our terrible repeating
Stupidities we used not sanction
The fears and doubts and trepidations
That marked the previous generation
So now in dealings with myself
I find I am constrained by health
Conditioned by the kind I have
As any one of Pavlov's horde
And whereas once my life was charmed
I am all too likely to come to harm
To fall while crying out loud
Constantly drowning in the crowd
To be detained for insobriety
For stumbling in Homeland Security
Or find I can no longer thole
The torments of passport control
The kind of fears I never had
When I was glad and mad and bad

But to return to what is true
My mother – off at eighty to Peru
Began to seem a little slow
To cut adrift and simply go
Until I put us on the spot
And asked: Are you afraid you'll drop?
And she said: Yes exactly that
That's what it is that has me stopped
And has me anxious in my head
The thought that I might drop down dead
So far away and so alone
And not a one to know or name

I could just as easy drop down here
But it's not the dying that I fear ...
Well if you drop you drop said I in turn
And you can stay or be brought home —
And sharply like a rope cut slack
'I think I'd rather be brought back'
As I swore she would whatever came
And that is how the deal was done

And Granda may go for a walk in the park
Separating light from dark
Reflecting how his time has gone
With everything each day brings on
Heroic maybe – but if so Mock
No serious speeching from the dock
But laughter and the same respect
As The Night Before poor Larry Was Stretched

January 2016